Previous Collections by Chas Addams

Chas Addams

MY CROWD

Simon and Schuster, New York

FIRST PRINTING

SBN 671-20788-1

LIBRARY OF CONGRESS CATALOG CARD NUMBER: 76-129192

MANUFACTURED IN THE UNITED STATES OF AMERICA

PRINTED BY THE HALLIDAY LITHOGRAPH CORPORATION, HANOVER, MASS.

BOUND BY AMERICAN BOOK-STRATFORD PRESS, INC., NEW YORK, N.Y.

Of the 189 drawings in this collection, 185 originally appeared in *The New Yorker* and were copyrighted © in 1937, 1939, 1940, 1942, 1946, 1948, 1949, 1950, 1951, 1952, 1953, 1954, 1955, 1956, 1957, 1958, 1959, 1960, 1961, 1962, 1963, 1964, 1965, 1966, 1967, 1968, and 1969 by The New Yorker Magazine, Inc.

To
James Geraghty

"*All your father can think of these days is politics.*"

"Now *maybe they'll be moved to do something about*
water pollution!"

"High tide, I see."

"*Tell me more about your husband, Mrs. Briggs.*"

1

3

2

4

"Nothing much, Agnes. What's new with you?"

"There's a silly sign if I ever saw one."

"*Oh, it's you! For a moment you gave me quite a start.*"

"Oh, my goodness, no! Just a water main."

"...then good old Scrooge, bless his heart, turned to Bob Cratchit and snarled, 'Let me hear another sound from you and you'll keep Christmas by losing your situation.'"

"It doesn't take much to collect a crowd in New York."

"Wallace, isn't that already too deep for glads?"

"I've been troubled lately by an eerie, recurring dream. I seem to be
seated in a darkened room staring in helpless fascination at some sort
of box, or cabinet, in the center of which is a phosphorescent likeness
of the human alimentary tract, rendered in graphic detail, while a
disembodied voice urges me to buy a potion for acid indigestion."

"There's enough hate in my heart for both of us."

"*Just a minute, you guys—we're missing one shovel.*"

"*It's the children, darling, back from camp.*"

"Well, Kendrick, still think I'm just an alarmist?"

"Suddenly, I have a dreadful urge to be merry."

"We won't be late, Miss Weems. Get the children to bed around
eight, and keep your back to the wall at all times."

"Your floor, sir."

"*Damnation, Forbes, stop looking at me like that.*"

"*Whatever the gods are, they aren't angry.*"

"*Goodness, Murray, it wouldn't be a picnic without ants.*"

1

2

3

4

5

6

7

8

9

10

11

12

"In addition to refusing to cultivate any wholesome interest in group activities, he is perverse, crafty, and wanton in those in which he does engage. These are, I feel impelled to emphasize, far beyond the outcroppings of normal juvenile mischief; in fact, they are the early evidences of what may be an extraordinarily morbid ingenuity. I have gone to such length in describing the situation because I know that you will want to be thoroughly informed of the facts."

"We never know what to expect when the leaves come down
in the fall."

"*Well, don't come whining to me. Go tell him you'll poison
him right back.*"

"*I think we're getting somewhere, Mr. Great Cloud Shadow. Your
neurosis apparently stems from a submerged resentment against
your ancestors for disposing of Manhattan Island for only
twenty-four dollars.*"

"Oh, go to sleep. I'll put up the screens in the morning."

"*Speak for yourself. Maybe you've had your day.*"

"Oh, speak up, George! Stop mumbling!"

"Ours is a very old family."

"Oh, for goodness' sake, forget it, Beasley. Play another one."

"*Then the dragon gobbled up the handsome young prince and his
lovely bride and lived happily ever after.*"

"*You needn't wrap it. I'll ride it home.*"

"All right, children, creative play period is over!"

"*That's strange. He wasn't part of the show at all.*"

"*Dearest: How I wish you were here with me now to see how lovely our little garden has become! The black nightshade is in full bloom, and the death camass we planted last fall is coming along beautifully. The henbane seems to have shot up overnight. You will be glad to know that the dwarf's hair was not affected by the dry spell, as we feared, after all. A myriad delightful little slugs have appeared, as if from nowhere, on the rotten stump by the belladonna patch, and this morning I noticed snake eggs hatching near the pool. Do finish up that business, darling, and hurry home.*"

"George! George! Drop the keys!"

"It's marvelous! All you do is add water."

"O.K. now. You got it straight what you're supposed to do?"

"*Bothered me a bit, too, at first, until I discovered they were real.*"

*"It may be none of my business, but there hasn't been a train over
that line in eight years."*

"Do you, Oliver Jordan III, take this woman to be your lawful wedded wife?"

"*Got a match, fella?*"

"*Dr. Fairburn is going to tell us about some of his interesting experiences among the head-shrinking tribes of Ecuador.*"

"Say, Donovan, do we have one with muffled oars?"

"*Are you unhappy, darling?*"

"*Oh, yes, yes! Completely.*"

"*Well, I don't see any point in looking any farther. It was probably just one of those wild rumors.*"

"Now, remember, you can have him as long as you feed him and take good care of him. When you don't, back he goes."

"We could never have done it without him."

"Now, let's just slip it on and see how it fits."

"Oh, I couldn't make it Friday—I've so many things to do.
It's the thirteenth, you know."

"Well, I'm ready if you are."

"You'll see, chicks, that half the fun is in making it yourself."

"Sorry, folks, we quit at five."

"We've had part of this floor finished off for Uncle Eimar."

"*Now kick Daddy good night and run along to bed.*"

"How would you like to be No. 1?"

"Have you got a minute, Dr. Headley? We think we may have found
a new carnivorous specimen."

"Darling!"

"*This is Uncle Zander. Grandfather always called him the black sheep.*"

1

2

5

6

3

4

7

8

"Just the kind of day that makes you feel good to be alive!"

"No, I don't know of any children's camp around here. Why?"

"*You see, children, I hate you both in* quite different *ways.*"

"May I borrow a cup of cyanide?"

"That? Oh, that's nothing. Just something I was fooling around with."

"It's a lovely spot—so unspoiled."

"Looks like Wesselman's hit on something interesting."

"*By George, you're right! I thought there was something familiar about it.*"

"*While you're here, there's a squeaky trap door I'd like you to look at.*"

"*This little piggy went to market,*
This little piggy stayed home,
This little piggy had roast beef,
This little piggy had none,
This little piggy went wee wee wee all the way home,
And this little piggy..."

"This is your room. If you should need anything, just scream."

"*Well, here's where I say good night.*"

"I've been thinking. This year, instead of giving *everything* away,
why don't we charge a little something?"

148

"Come along, children—time for your nap."

"I give up, Robert. What does have two horns, one eye, and creeps?"

"Sanders speaking. Stop all production on XP 15, recall all shipments, wire every doctor in the country, and hurry!"

"But how do I know you're an enchanted prince?"

"Mr. Mitchell! You know you don't have kitchen privileges."

"I'm sorry, sonny. We've run out of candy."

"All right, children, a nice big sneer, now."

"You forgot the eye of newt."

"Reminds one of a patchwork quilt, doesn't it?"

*"Now... Listen to the shriek run through its entire range
without peaking."*

"What light you giving it?"

"It's priceless. *Normie's building a rocket to shoot Pamela*
to the moon."

"*We're not living happily ever after.*"

"You're going to shoot a hundred and fourteen, dear."

"Who ordered the fish?"

"The little dears! They still believe in Santa Claus."

"Can't you get along with anybody?"

"*Death ray, fiddlesticks! Why it doesn't even slow them up.*"

"I've heard that outside of working hours he's really a
rather decent sort."

"...and if it's a boy, we're going to give him a Biblical name,
like Cain or Ananias."

"All right, now, a little smile."

"*I like them. They wear* well."

"Personally, I can't imagine what he sees in her."